How to Install Kodi on Firestick:

The 2017 Step-by-Step Edition
(beginner to expert level guide)
Tips and Tricks for ANY user included

Table of Contents

Introduction

Congratulations on downloading this book and thank you for doing so.

The following chapters will discuss the right way for you to install Kodi on your Firestick and how to make sure that you are getting the most out of it each time that use the Kodi application. There are so many tips that come along with this book, you should have no problem being able to use Kodi in any way that you like.

There are plenty of books on this subject on the market, thanks again for choosing this one! Every effort was made to ensure it is full of as much useful information as possible, please enjoy!

Chapter 1: Learn About Kodi

Kodi is an application that can be used to connect to many different file-sharing and streaming sites. It allows you to stream music, movies, TV shows and other popular, interesting attractions to practically any device, including your Firestick. Since it is open source, you can make use of it on any type of platform, and you will be able to rest assured that at the end of the day, you can just look at the source code and feel secure that you're using a safe application. There are many different things that you can do with Kodi but, at the core, it can be used for entertainment.

Various Uses
The Kodi enables you to do different things with all of the mass media sources that you have. You can watch TV shows, view movies, and even look at pictures by using it. Because of the functions that it has, it gives you everything that you will need to get started and get on the path to having a powerful media center right on your Firestick. Also, it is a great addition to the several types of streaming devices that are available on the market. With Kodi, you will be able to take full advantage about the device that you have even if it does indeed not normally link up with the movie or music you are striving to view or listen to.

When it comes to movies, Kodi can get them from different places. There are different options for you when you want to watch films. You can choose the movie that you would like to watch right from the Kodi mobile app and watch as it is played on your device. This is especially beneficial if you have a device that won't natively allow you to play certain file types. It is a great addition to any type of set-up, and you will be able to get various movies right on the Kodi app.

Since the mobile app is capable of being used with practically any type of media, you can even put your own pictures and music into it. This is a great option if you need to show off different pictures that you have or if you want to use your streaming device as a virtual jukebox. It isn't just about movies and television shows like several of the other kinds of software that exist - it's about every type of media.

Kodi on Firestick
One of the sweetest parts about using the Kodi software is that it can be installed and used straight on your Firestick. In the past, users of the Firestick were limited to simply a few options for media. They'd have to make certain that they were in a position to get the multimedia from Amazon or one of the other programs that the Firestick recognized; nevertheless, with Kodi, they are able to watch music and movies even if they happen to be not on one of the supported programs.

Unlike several of the other things that are included with the Firestick, you will be required to manually install Kodi onto your Firestick if you're wanting to use it. There are many options for this, and it will change the way that you do different things. You can make sure you are getting the best of the Firestick and Kodi blend by just making certain you are using it to get movies and television shows that you wouldn't typically be able to get – which, trust me, Kodi turns into a breeze. When you have downloaded the Kodi app, you will not be concerned about what application or service has the movie that you're wanting to watch. *Everything* will route through Kodi.

Once you have installed the Kodi on your Firestick, working with and making use of it is incredibly straightforward. You will just need to create an account that can be used and you will be in a position to stream all of the movies and the TV shows that you would like. Establishing an account is even simpler than some of the other streaming services, so it is merely one less step that you'll need to worry about.

Once you have completed all of this, there are other things that you will need to do. You should work to make certain that Kodi is going to be able to meet your needs and that you are going to be getting the most out of the app, for example.

Essential Files
There are a few programs that you can download for your Firestick that require you to download specific files, but Kodi has the capacity to work with the files that are included in different popular features of the app. The only thing that you will have to do is be sure that your Firestick is going to allow software from unknown sources by doing the following:
1. Go to Settings
2. Select the system option
3. "Developer Options."
4. Toggle the button for "apps from unknown sources" to on
5. Return to Settings
6. Put the IP in for the Kodi software
7. Download
8. Use Kodi! Enjoy!

Also, you can download it through the Internet, but this process is slightly different. In the event that you are going to use the browser that is included with your Firestick, you will need to first make sure that you are allowing the programs from unidentified sources to be downloaded (like you did with the other install option) and then download the files that coordinate with different options that are included on the Firestick. It will give you a chance to be sure that you are getting what you need from the Firestick and that you can make certain that the mobile app is being downloaded the right way. If you utilize this option, make sure that you include all of the files that are required so that you can run the app.

Once the software is installed on your device, you will be able to put it to use to watch the television and movies that you love. You will additionally be able to upload your own photographs and music to it, meaning you get to take full advantage of any existing media libraries you have. There is a huge number of different options that Kodi offers to you, and you're going to have a lot of fun exploring them.

Features of Kodi
The Kodi mobile app always has a lot of great features that allow you the chance to make certain that you will be able to truly make the most of all of your media library, but the latest version has recently been improved even more to make certain that you have all of the features that you need. The advancements that are included with Kodi incorporate some of the best new features. The latest version has:
- 3D video playlists
- Seeking through different elements of a movie or a TV program
- New closed captioning
- Accessibility adjustments that can be transformed and updated
- New look which allows the mobile app to look more attractive without changing any functionality to it

All of these features are in addition to what Kodi was able to do before and are included with the latest software update to enable you to put it to use to make certain that you are taking benefits of the insights in it. Kodi is a beautiful, living piece of software that is updated, changed, and made better with every single new release, and making sure you keep Kodi up to date lends you the possibility to be sure that you are getting the most out of the experience.

With Kodi, you can do practically anything that you want with the music and the movies that you adore. Not only can you simply watch a film like you would be able to do on any other streaming service - you can also fast-forward, rewind, and pause them when you need to. This is made easier by the extra features of Kodi.

Not merely are you able to do this but you are also able to make certain you happen to be doing it with the most convenience to yourself. Kodi now supports up to a 10-foot range so as to make use of it when you aren't right next to the device that you are streaming to. This is suitable for use with most remotes and makes sure that you are getting the most out of the experience. This makes working with and using your Kodi extremely simple and convenient.

Chapter 2: Getting Kodi on Your Firestick

As the process of installing Kodi seems relatively simple if you are going to be using it on your Firestick, there are a few steps that you will need to take to make certain that you are getting the most out of it. You are going to be able to put it to use in combination with the Firestick's preexisting capabilities, as I've already said. You should make sure that you follow these instructions each time that you will be using your Firestick so that you will have the best experience possible and will also be able to be sure that you are taking advantage of the features within it.

Setting up from Different Platforms

Seeing that the Kodi is so versatile, you may use different options to be able to install it on your Firestick. You can do this through the several platforms that you have accessible to you, and it will allow you the chance to be sure that you are getting the most from your Firestick as well as your Kodi app. When you set up the Kodi mobile app on your Firestick, you can use an internet browser, a mobile device or other less conventional options to install it.

The main thing that you need to do when you are installing it is make sure that you have both the chosen platform and the Firestick operating on the same network. This is the only way that they will be linked together, and you will only be able to use the app install information if you have them on the same network. Make certain that they are both on your home wi-fi network and the one which you will be using at all times when you are using the Firestick. If this is your first time using the Firestick, you will need to undergo the setup process to ensure that it is linked to the right network.

You should always make sure that both the platform and the Firestick are going to accept the app. You need to make certain that both of them are going allow software to be downloaded from unknown resources. You will not be able to make the mobile app work on your Firestick should you not do this first and you may have trouble getting started out with the several options that are included in the software if you are not able to accomplish this.

Step-by-step

You need to first make sure that your Firestick is on your TV. Plug it in your USB port that you want to use all of the time so that you do not have to be anxious about unplugging it and then plugging it in once more when you are done configuring it for use with Kodi. You should have already configured your Firestick to be hooked up to your network, and you should have already tried it for watching TV.

When you have plugged it in and made sure it is operating properly, you will need to go to the configurations section. From there, click on the system options and then after, click the developer options button. This will allow you to see all of the different actions that you can carry out with Firestick to be sure you happen to be getting the most out of the device. Where the option says "apps from unknown sources" and "ADB debugging", use the toggle move to change both of these to "ON" so as to make sure that you are getting the most out of the options and that you can then be capable of connecting it to your Kodi app.

After you have ensured that both of these options are recorded, go back to the options to "about" and then click on the network option. Right there on the screen is the IP address of your Firestick. Keep this open up so that you have it on hand or record it to enable you to look at it during the next thing.

Open a browser on your desktop or your laptop computer and find the Android APK data file. This is on the Kodi website, and you could download it right from there. After that, you will also be able to download the file, and then you will want to open it back up to click a "new" tab. Create a name for your Firestick and then put the IP address that you obtained earlier into the address bar. Save it so that you will not need to come back later. After it is preserved, click on the connection button so as to hook up your Firestick to the application. You should know that it is linked when it comes up in the set of "connected" devices. Very well, on to the next step.

Go to that list and click on it. You will then have the option to click on the "Install APK" which will supply you with the chance to make certain that you are installing and downloading Kodi. When you are asked if you'd like to install it, you should click yes, and then you will need to click OK.

It doesn't matter matter what device you have done it from or what platform you will work off of, you will now have Kodi on your Firestick. This pretty much can be done with any laptop or personal PC that uses any operating system.

Keep in mind that this may well not work for each and every time that you make an effort to download Kodi. If you find it is not working, you can then go to the previous section and try that method of downloading it. It is a great idea to try different things until you find the software and the settings that are going to work for you. Your Firestick may have different configurations than what others do, and you may struggle to find that there are different things that you will do when you are downloading Kodi on your Firestick.

Using Kodi
When you have downloaded Kodi the first time, it may seem rather complicated for you to use, especially if you aren't tech savvy or explorative. You may want to set some time aside and try different things as you are learning how to put it to use that will help you to figure away all of the details of it. It might not exactly be as easy as you were thinking so you should try different options if you are first getting started.

If you have never used Kodi before, you should utilize the Kodi website to find the several options you can do. All of these options are things that will make it easier that you can make use of it and will give you some idea of the right way to navigate the software while you are using your Firestick. The website should have everything that you must know about Kodi and will provide you with all of the information how to navigate the application and how to be sure that it is working with your Firestick.

If there are any problems with your Kodi application, there are a few things that you may like to do to troubleshoot it:
- Make sure that the software is up to date to where it needs to be
- Check to be sure that your Firestick is connected
- Test the network connection that the Firestick is on
- Look at your configurations on your Firestick and ensure both of them are set to the "ON" setting and that absolutely nothing has been reset

Ideas for Kodi
Since Kodi is free, there are many different options that are included in the application and all of the media possibilities bundled therein. You can find practically anything at all that you want to watch while you are using the application and you could even download your own media to it to enable you to try various things. Make sure that you are using it as often as possible when you have it linked to your Firestick.

There are numerous options that come together with Kodi. Try to find the application options that work for you. Apart from making sure that it is connected to your Firestick, the applied options can be completely custom-made, and that is something that will enable you to ensure that your Kodi is functioning with your Firestick.

If you need to find movies or TV shows that you just can't seem to locate on Kodi, you will need to download them yourself on your computer. From there, you can put them on the file that you have already created for your Kodi, and it will give you a chance to be positive that you are getting the most out of the device. While there are many movies and TV shows that you can download right from the app, some of the less popular options may not be easily accessible for you.

Chapter 3: The Easiest Way to Download Kodi

There are some instances that may be different from others. These can include needing to download Kodi without having a computer useful, needing to upgrade to a different version of Kodi, and trying to ensure that you are getting the most out of each of the things that you can do with Kodi. While you may not necessarily need any of these options when you are first getting started with Kodi for Firestick, you may want to bear them in mind for a future date when you do. They may help you to have a better experience with Kodi and will give you options that you did not find out about in the previous chapters.

Direct Download

Should you not have a computer available or something that you can use to be able to download Kodi, there is a way around it. Downloading the program is much less simple that it would be with a computer but it will still allow you to use it. If you do, indeed, have a computer, it could be a good idea to avoid this option because it is not the most stable option and can cause problems with your Firestick device.

Start out by turning your Firestick on and making sure that all of the ADB, USB, and APPS buttons are switched to the "ON" position as you were in the earlier steps. While it should be connected already, double check to ensure that it is in the network that you use for your wi-fi and that the signal is strong.

Go to the search menu of your Firestick and enter ES explorer. Press the enter button and then go ahead and try to find the application. The ES Explorer will be in the final results and will have a blue image that will look similar to the one that you would normally see on a computer. You can then simply click it to download it, and it will then be available for you to use on your Firestick. After you are sure that it offers completely downloaded, open up it up.

You will now be able to use the ES Explorer on your Firestick exactly how you did it on your computer. Move to the Kodi website and download it. Click on the Path button and then make the name to it. Add it to your bookmarks and then open up it up. Utilize the up and down keys to make sure that you can get through the page. Press the button that states "Download", and it will open up different options, including the option for downloading to Android. You can then pick the "more" button that lies below PROVIDE that is underneath Android. Select the option that allows you to be open it in your web browser.

If you want to be able to use your Kodi application on your Firestick, you will need the Fire Starter software to help you organize all of the software that you have saved. You can find Firestarter by going to the same explorer browser and putting it into the browser. The download process for Fire Starter is the same as it was for Kodi. As soon as you have installed Open Fire Starter, you will be able to see that there are now different files on your Firestick and that they all match to the various open source applications that you have downloaded. Fire Starter and Kodi will both take the folders and the list of apps.

There are also other applications that you can download to make your Kodi device more effective and find numerous music, movie, and television shows. This will enable you to get the best use of your device and will make things better for both your device and you. The Fusion software is the one that you can get that will allow you to find even more music and movies. All the applications that you get as open source programs will be performed in the same way that you did the Kodi software and the subsequent Fire Starter app. They will make your experience with Kodi better, more seamless and more optimized to your device.

Upgrading to a PC
The easiest way that you can update or upgrade the Kodi application that you have on your Firestick is to do so from a computer so that you will be able to get the best options possible out of it and that you will not have to consider what you are doing with your Firestick. This will give you an opportunity to make certain that you are getting the most out of the application.

After you have made sure that your Firestick will be able to accept downloading from unknown sources, you will need to available up to a browser on your computer. Ensure that you have the APK installed on the computer, too, so that you will be able to download the upgrade in a similar way to how you downloaded the application originally. Set up the downloaded from the home page.

Go to your browser and put the Kodi URL into the form to put web addresses. This will allow one to see different options and download the information that you need for your Kodi. The website will have a section for upgrades. There, you can examine and see if you have the latest version of Kodi or if you need to update.

You can then click on the install button. As long as your Kodi, as well as your computer, are on the same network, your Kodi will be able to accept the improvements which were put into the downloader on your PC. Check your Kodi on your Firestick to be sure that the update has been installed.

Updating with No PC
Unless you have a PC available or you are unable to utilize it to be able to get the upgrades to Kodi on your Firestick, you may need to do it without the computer and just on the Firestick alone. This will allow you the chance to be sure that you are permitting yourself to do the complete download that is included with the Firestick. It will give you more options than just doing it on the computer.

As with every other option with Kodi, you need to make certain that your Firestick is able to accept programs from unidentified sources by toggling to the "ON" button.

In case you have downloaded the software before using the ES Explorer, you will currently have it on your Firestick. If you have not, you will need to obtain the ES Explorer on the search button of the Firestick and get it to be able to utilize it to do the rest of the steps.

After you have downloaded it and it is on your Firestick, you should be able to then open it up and navigate to the Kodi website. Find the upgrade section and update using the Android settings. It should take some time to install so ensure that your network connection is strong.

Once the installation is complete, check your Firestick to make certain that your settings are not changed but that your Kodi has been installed and updated to the latest version. Go with your Kodi in the same way that you normally would.

You will find not many changes are made to Kodi on a regular schedule so you should not have to update the program over and over. Mostly, the Kodi releases are rather gradual and slow-coming, meaning that you can for the most part relax and just enjoy the Kodi ride. You should always examine the website first to see if it comes with an upgrade available. Anytime there is an upgrade, you need to ensure that you are doing the upgrade so that you are able to get the best system possible and get the most out of the functions that are being done on the system. It is just a good idea to do the upgrades as they are released so that you will get the most out of it.

Kodi has many different facets that make up the several elements of the application. There could be upgrades to each of the various parts that will help you to have a much better time at using the application. By doing the upgrades that you need to do to it, you will not only allow yourself to have access to more options, but you will also allow your Kodi to be able to function at the maximum capacity which it can. The more that are upgraded, the better it will work and the more chance you have at making sure that you can get things done the proper way. If you are using your Kodi, it is recommended to make sure that you are also upgrading it so that the program is up to date as much as possible. You may find that there are more movies, TV shows and other media that you should enjoy when you do the upgrades on a regular basis.

Chapter 4: Adding On to Kodi and Wizards

Just because you have Kodi and it is able to work well with your Firestick really does not mean that you won't need other applications to help you make use of it the right way. Your current Kodi application will be able to function more easily if you are getting the best of it with various add-ons and wizards that will help you with different things when it comes to your Kodi. Typically the way that you utilize each of these things will make it easier so that you can get the most out of your Kodi and will give you the possibility to do more with Kodi. It will make your viewing experience better and will also allow you the chance to do more with the Firestick that you have.

Add-Ons

These are things which you can use to make your experience with Kodi better. They will work with almost anything at all that you want to do with Kodi and will give you a chance to make certain that you are getting the most out of your software. They may be used for watching movies, television shows, and other similar forms of media. The add-ons are third party applications that can be downloaded similarly to how you actually downloaded Kodi. It is a good idea to use these ones to get the most from the viewing experience.

Pro Sports - When you want to be able to watch sports activities or sport related events on your Kodi application, you will need the Pro Sports application. That will allow you to see both life and leading sports events. There are many options that you can choose from, and you could even watch online games which have been archived. It really is like having your own sports channel on demand at any time that you want.

SALTS - There are many different television shows that are added to this application. It offers the information that you need for TV shows and has some of the most recent and most popular shows. This is actually the application that you should use when you are using Kodi, and you cannot find the television show that you are looking for on any other form of application for your Firestick. It will allow you to find the perfect show, regardless of what you want to watch.

123Movies - This add-on is great for individuals who are just getting to grips with their Kodi and the several applications that can be used along with it. All you need to do is click to download and then you will be able to make use of it to your full advantage. There are not many other programs like this that are so simple to operate so take benefit of this. It is a great beginner option and is used regardless of what you have on your Kodi or what other applications you choose to use each time that you are doing different things.

iStream - You can use this add-on to find different movies and television shows. It is user run, and all of the information that is on it has been put there by users. It can be used in combination with Kodi along with many other apps so that you can afford to make certain that you are getting the most out of it. It is straightforward to use, has a lot of content, and even has some obscure shows that you might not be able to find on any other application or device that you have available to use with your Kodi.

Redemption - If you are looking for a program that can be used as an all in one add on, you will want to go for Redemption. This add-on allows you to find TV, music, movies, and any other types of media that you may want. It will give you a chance to ensure that you are getting the most out of the wide breadth of information and media out there, and that your Kodi is able to be used easily. Presently there are different options for Redemption, but the best ones include all of the information that you need to be able to put the right things together with your Kodi application.

Stream Hub - Everyone is able to find something that they love about Supply Hub. While the greater part of the content is intended for many different people, it has sections that are particularly for adults. This specifically is one of the only reliable applications that can be used for this purpose, and it is able to be utilized in combo with your Kodi. It is a good idea to try to figure out the right way to use this and the various options that are incorporated with it each time that you want to put more files in your Kodi program.

BOB - There are numerous users who make up the database of BOB. The people who run this add-on are accountable for adding content to it and will do so on a regular basis. This user-run add-on is great for folks who want to be able to get a lot of different content options and who want to be able to get more than average tv set shows and films that are normally found on Kodi and the succeeding add-ons into it. You can choose from different things that will be added to Kodi when you are able to use the BOB add-on.

Exodus - As one of the premier options for folks who use Kodi, Exodus has been around for almost as long as Kodi has been. It has some of the most popular TV shows and movies along with the several options that are incorporated into it. You can make certain you are able to get the most content with Exodus by upgrading it on a regular basis. It will allow you the chance to be sure that you are getting the most out of the application and you can get the best TV shows and movies on your Kodi application through your Firestick.

One thing that you should remember is that adult content add-ons can be harmful to your Kodi program and then for your Firestick in general. You have to ensure that you are using the add-ons in the way that make sense and using ones which have various content will be your best gamble even though you are looking for adult content. The ones that are intended for that objective only do not usually have a strong infrastructure, are not updated regularly, and can be detrimental to your Firestick.

Wizards

In case you have been using Kodi for a while, and you want to be able to get more out there of the application and the add-ons that you have included with the application, the Wizards are your best options for the several things that you can do. They are able to pull information from the add-ons, plus they can incorporate each of them collectively to get what you need out from the application process. Despite the fact that the add-ons are great, the wizards are even better because they take increase the utility that the add-ons have to give you.

Hard Nox - No matter what add-ons you have on your Kodi, you may use this wizard to be able to find all of the information that you need from each of them. You should make sure that you are getting the most out of the process and that you are able to search for each and every of the options that are included with the add-ons. You can simply do this by getting Hard Nox and doing it search that is incorporated into it to find the information or the show, movie or music that you would like.

Schism - As an all-in-one wizard, it is hard to beat Schism. This includes everything that you need in order to make your Kodi suite run on all cylinders. It enables you to look at different options, learn the various items and add different things to your Kodi. It will also give you the chance to ensure that you are doing the most with it and that you are getting the most out of it. You do not even need to get the add-ons to use this wizard because it is an all in one wizard.

Tomb Raider - This can be a great option for folks that are just getting started with their Kodi and with the subsequent add-ons that come along with it. This will allow you the chance to be sure that you are getting the most out of it, that you can modify your Kodi to make things look better when it comes to adding your information and files onto Kodi. That will also allow you the chance to find out more about add-ons, wizards, and the way that both of these things work with your Kodi on your Firestick.

Chapter 5: Problems You May Encounter with Kodi

While keeping your Kodi upgraded and making sure that you are becoming the most use out of it are the easiest things that you can do to make certain that your Kodi is working the best for you, you should also be sure that you are getting the best of the device and that you are able to solve all of the problems that come along with the device. There should not be too many issues that you have with your Kodi but knowing the most frequent mistakes and how you can troubleshoot errors will enable you to make certain that you are getting the most out of your Kodi.

Common Mistakes
The most typical mistakes are usually simple fixes. Nevertheless, they are something that you might not exactly even know about. Some users simply choose to ignore the problems or the mistakes if they are unable to solve them straight away which can lead to them not employing their Kodi application to its full advantage. As long as you really know what the most typical errors are, what exactly they are caused by, and how you can fix them, you will be able to figure out a way to ensure that your Kodi is working in the best way possible.

As the majority of the Kodi problems are simple fixes, there is no single way that you can fix all of them or prevent them. It will not be possible to prevent all of the issues that come along with your Kodi application. Instead, you need to really know what you can do to be sure that you can to fix them when they actually happen.

Network Problem - This is the most typical error that folks receive when they are using the Kodi application, and it can be tough to figure out there what the error is. It is something that they have to ensure that they are doing the right way and they also want to make certain that the Kodi is linked to the network that their Firestick is on. In the case you are not on the same network, you will have problems with connectivity and also get all of the playback options on your Kodi application.

After you have made sure that the condition really does not come from your reference to the device and your network, you should make sure that your connection is as optimized as possible. You need to see how strong your network is, check it to ensure that it is truly linked to the Internet and see what the signal is like. This could be the condition for many of the issues you have with Kodi and is frequently simple as resetting your network to ensure that you are getting the most out of it. You needs to be certain that you will be getting the best network signal and that things are being done the right way on your network.

Failed Playback - The most typical reason for a failed playback is that your Kodi is not interacting properly with any of the third-party applications that you have installed on your Firestick. Since there is no support for making sure that the software is bonding, you will need to ensure you are getting the most out of the software process and that you are able to have what you need as it pertains to the several apps. Check to make certain that your third-party applications are functioning and that they are upgraded to the point that you want those to be if you wish to be sure that they are interacting with Kodi.

If the software is up to date and the situation continues to show up on your Kodi application, you will simply need to evaluate the "OK" button because it will allow you to proceed from the error message and just get on the show or the movie that you are seeking to play.

Spinning Circle - When you see a spinning circle on the screen of your Kodi, it essentially means that the mobile app is "thinking" or interacting with your Firestick. It will really make a difference in the way that things are done and the playback abilities that the device allows, but you should always make sure that you are getting the most out of it and that you let it continue to spin if you are doing different things. If you want to accelerate the process, you can consider examining your network to be sure that there are no issues with it. Another option that you will have when it comes to your Kodi device is to just move the network a little nearer. This could help to speed up the way that the Kodi interacts with your Firestick.

If you continue to end up having it rotating or taking too long to figure out what you want it to do, you can consider upgrading your network and getting something that has faster speeds. This will allow the chance to make certain that the speed is fast enough and that you are getting the most out of it. This often involves a straightforward call to your Web provider, and you will then be able to benefit from a more powerful network and faster speeds.

Simply No Stream Available - This is not uncommon to see this message when you are trying to watch a show or a TV. You may also see this when you are simply browsing through the various areas and also the precise product information that is available so that you can look at. If you find out that there is no stream available, you will need to look at your third party apps. This is almost always the reason for this error and is changed depending on what you need to do with the applications. Check the programs to ensure that they are working and that you are going to be able to get the most out of them.

You should also ensure that they are updated, that they have not been removed from your Firestick and that they are functioning properly. If none of these is the problem, the software may simply not be working. All you should do when this happens is delete the phone app from the Firestick and re-add it to the applications which you have. This will allow you the chance to make certain that you are getting the most out of it and that you are able to include all of the extras that come along with the app.

Troubleshooting Your Kodi
The application will not come with a lot of support, but there are a few things that you should make sure of before you try something else. There are some methods to basic problems that can be found on the Kodi website, but you can avoid having to do this if you just do these things when you notice that there may be a problem with the application.

Plug it in - The Firestick should always be plugged into your device before making the decision to use Kodi. In case it is not properly plugged in, you will not be able to use Kodi, and you will not be able to get the full advantage out of it. Even if you feel that your Firestick is connected, you should still check it in case it was pulled out or it is coming loose from the plug. There are several opportunities that such a thing could happen. If it is blocked by your device, consider unplugging it and then plugging it back in. Occasionally this is plenty to totally reset it, allowing Kodi to work properly.

Check the connection - Even if you feel that your Internet connection is working properly, you may need to ensure that it must be working the right way and that it is as fast as possible. Bad weather, furniture getting in the way or a router that is too significantly away can all cause problems with the Internet connection. You have to just make sure that none of these are generally triggering problems with your Internet connection so that you will be able to get the best benefit out of Kodi and the way that it works with your Firestick.

Use your computer - the computer that you place your Kodi device after may be the best option that you have for troubleshooting. Regardless of whether you decided to use the mobile app or use a browser, you should check that to make certain that there are no problems with it. You may log into the mobile app trying to do different things. Take a look at the several options that the Kodi has. If you find that there are issues, it might be the time that you should upgrade your Kodi so that it works the right way - some upgrades are done to remove small issues with cable connections and other things.

Chapter 6: Sequence of Addition Matters

Since there are different methods for downloading Kodi for your Firestick, there are factors to consider that you are doing the same thing for each and every of the methods. The order in which you do the download will help you to ensure that you are taking advantage of the insights in the situation and that you are going to be in a position to include everything that you need on your Firestick. It is imperative that you have the order down and that you really know what you are doing so you do not risk damaging your Firestick.

The Order

The first thing that you will need to do is ensure that you are linked to the same network on your device and on the computer that you will be downloading Kodi on. This is not hard to do if you only have access to one network on your computer or your device but may be more complicated when there are several different networks that are near you or that show up in your home. It is necessary to be sure that you are on the right network and one with the strongest transmission so that you will be able to make the connection between the Firestick, the Kodi application and the device you are downloading everything on. This is just what you need to do to get the most out from the Kodi application as well as your Firestick device.

After you have done this step, you will then need to ensure that your Firestick is on. You should not download Kodi unless of course, your Firestick is on. If you do get it and the Firestick is not on, you will likely have to go through the entire process again to be sure that you have the software on your Firestick. This will allow you the chance to ensure that you are getting the most out of it and that you are not wasting your time with a second download.

The rest of the steps do not require a specific sequence, but it is better to be sure that you are taking advantage of the insights in the application each time that you download it. Despite the fact that the order does not matter, you still should do each of the steps. If you are not able to include all of the information with your Firestick device, you will not be able to get the most out there of the as well as the application of an effect.

Changes

There will occasionally be changes that you will need to make on your Kodi application. This could be anything from making sure that the software is installed properly to doing the upgrades that are required to keep the software working in the best way possible. When you make changes to Kodi, you will also need to make certain that those changes are included in your Firestick device. Your small changes will need to take effect on the Firestick, and you will need to make certain that you are taking advantage of the insights in the Kodi application.

While you find out more on the Firestick, your Kodi application and all of the things that go into the application, you will be able to help make the changes that you need. It is important that you add different things to your device and that you are getting the most out of it each time that you benefit different things.

To make sure that your changes are updating on your Firestick when you update your Kodi application, you will just need to look at the various things that are offered on the Firestick and the Kodi application. It is important to remember what the Kodi application was like before the changes were made. Compare that to what is on your Firestick so you can make sure that your Kodi application has updated on your PC as well as on your Firestick.

Adding Information

When you first sign up for Kodi, you will need to put some information into the application. This is merely basic information that will explain to the application a little about you, what you like, and what you are considering watching on the device. As you have the device, you may find that you would like more out of it and that you will probably be able to get the best experience possible. You can add additional information to your Kodi application each time that you log in. While you might not be able to do everything that you want to Kodi without the wizards installed on it, you can add the information to your application through your computer. This is important if you need to get the most out of the application and if you wish to include everything in the application.

This is a good idea to try to add as much information as you can to Kodi while you are first setting it up. This will save you from having to go again down the road and put that information in, and it will also allow you the possibility to ensure that the software is flawlessly matched to all of your settings, interests, and everything that you want it to add. You can try different things with the app, but the best decision is to be sure that you include all of the relevant information.

Benefits of the Right Order

When you download your Kodi application, you should make sure that you are getting the most out of the application. To be able to do this, you will need to make sure that you are getting the most out of it and that you are doing more with it. This is something that will set your Kodi application. There are so many issues that come along with having the application that you must make sure that you are doing it the right way and that you are using all of the right things to ensure that you are getting the most out of your Kodi application.

Since it is something that needs to be downloaded differently from other applications that you would download on your Firestick, you should always be doing it in a way that makes sense, and the correct manner is suggested by the Kodi site. It is important that you do it in the right order so that you will not have problems with your Kodi and so that you will be able to get the most out of the Kodi.

Making sure that each of the ways that you download the Kodi application and each of the steps is followed exactly will give you a chance to be able to have the app work in the best way possible on your Firestick. This is essential to your Firestick and will allow you to get the most usage out of your Kodi application. Each time that you do different things with your Kodi, you will be able to do the most with it.

Updating the Kodi Application
While it is far more likely that you will need to update your Firestick more often than your Kodi application, there are still some things that you will need to do to make sure that your Kodi is up to date. Whether you regularly update it or not will depend on how often you visit the Kodi site. It can make a difference to whether or not you are able to work with the app or whether you need to update it to be able to do different things. It is always a good idea to try more with your Kodi app so that you will be able to get the most out of it.

If you are working on different things with Kodi, you will need to be able to update it. There is a reason that the publishers create the software updates and want you to get them. The majority of updates that are included with your Kodi software have things like changes to the way that the application functions, options to make it look better, additions to allow it the chance to perform more smoothly, and updates that will help with the security of the application when it is being used on your Firestick.

Kodi Changes
Each time that there is a software update to your Kodi application, there will likely be some changes that are made to it. This can be anything from minor changes – like the way that the app looks or the skins that are included with the app – to major changes like performance options that are included. It is important to always do the updates so that you will be able to take advantage of each of the things that are included in the application.

Add-On Changes
When you are doing different things with your Kodi, you need to make sure that you are updating it in the right way. There are many different options that can be included with your Kodi application. When you are doing updates to the application, you may not be able to do different things with your add-ons. You should always make sure that your add-ons are still working with your Kodi application and with the Firestick device that you are using. Updates to Firestick and Kodi can both make it more difficult for the add-ons to work in the way that they are supposed to.

Chapter 7: Links and Helpful Suggestions

When you are downloading Kodi for your Firestick, you may find that there are a few things that you need to make sure that you are doing. Each of these things has an internet link which corresponds to it, and it is important that you make sure that you are using the links so that you will be able to get everything that you need. It will allow you to have a better experience with the Firestick application and will also make things go more smoothly when you are working to get what you need out of Kodi. There are many different options that you can use, but the links that are included are the most commonly used ones and the ones that will allow you the chance to make sure that you are getting the most out of the Kodi for Firestick application.

The best links to use:

Kodi Downloader (this will be needed no matter where you are trying to download the application to) - https://kodi.tv/download/

APK Download necessary for installation on the Firestick - https://apkpure.com/

The downloading tool that is necessary for use with the APK download - https://www.apk4fun.com/apk/16712/

Various Kodi add-ons - http://addons.kodi.tv/

Tips and Tricks

To make sure that you are getting the best experience out of your Kodi, you need to make sure that you are following all of the tips and tricks that come along with the device. This is something that will allow you the chance to make sure that your Kodi device is working in the best way possible and that you are getting the most out of it. When you are working to make sure that your Kodi is working, you will give yourself the best chance at having a good experience. No matter what you do, you need to make sure that you are trying your best to be able to get the media that you want on Kodi.

Updated Versions
To download Kodi or any of the add-ons that come with Kodi, you will need to make sure that your Firestick is up to date. There are many different options with the Firestick, and each of them is different depending on what you are able to do with your specific Firestick. It is important that you make sure that you are downloading all of the software updates and that you are doing it in a way that allows you the chance to see that there are new things available. This should be done the first time that you try to download Kodi for your Firestick.

It is also important to note that you will need to do this each time that there is an update on Firestick. The Firestick software has new changes and updates that are added to it on a regular basis and, if you do not do them, you risk not only being able to use your Kodi application in the way that you want but also using your entire Firestick.

Always Use the Firestick
Your Firestick is going to give you everything that you need for your Kodi. This means that you need to make sure that your Kodi is up to date and that it will function with your Firestick. You should also make sure that you will be giving yourself the best option possible and that you are getting everything that you can out of the Kodi.

Firestick Troubleshooting
If there is something wrong with your Kodi or you think that it is not working properly with your Firestick, you should first assume that it might be your Firestick instead of the Kodi application. While there is a chance that you are going to have problems with your Kodi, there is a higher chance that you will have problems with Firestick and you must first work to make sure that you are getting the most out of this. It will also be easier for you to update to a new version of Firestick than it will be for you to try to update to a new version of Kodi. This is because the process for updating to Firestick is much easier and more streamlined than trying to make sure that you are updating the right way to your Kodi device. Depending on the way that you want to be able to get the most out of your Kodi, you will need to try to update to the Firestick software before you can use Kodi.

Security
No matter what you want to do with your Kodi Application and the things that you have included with it, you need to make sure that you are always maintaining the highest level of security possible. This will help you to protect your Firestick and any of the personal information. While Kodi is generally regarded as a safe application for you to use when it comes to your Firestick, you need to make sure that you are not going to encounter any problems that may come along with it, too. Make sure that you only download it from the actual Kodi source. You should also be careful with your add-ons because some of them may not be coming from the best sources. You should always make sure that you download only the add-ons that make sense and that are recommended by Kodi so that you will be able to get the best experience possible for your Kodi application and avoid compromising your device.

There are so many benefits that come along with using your Kodi device. By taking advantage of each of these benefits, you will be giving yourself the best option possible for your Kodi and your Firestick. Make sure that you are always careful with your Kodi application and that you do the best job possible when downloading so that you are able to get all of the shows, music, and movies that you want.

Conclusion

Thank for making it through to the end of this book, let's hope it was informative and able to provide you with all of the tools you need to achieve your goals whatever they may be.

The next step is to download Kodi for your Firestick. Now that you have seen all of the installation information, you should not have a problem installing it and getting on the fast track to having your very own one-stop media hub.

Finally, if you found this book useful in any way, a review on Amazon is always appreciated!